A CourseGuide for

Five Views on
Biblical
Inerrancy

J. Merrick, Stephan M. Garrett
Editors

R. Albert Mohler Jr., Peter Enns, Michael F. Bird,
Kevin J. Vanhoozer, John R. Franke
Contributors

**ZONDERVAN
ACADEMIC**

ZONDERVAN ACADEMIC

A CourseGuide for Five Views on Biblical Inerrancy

Copyright © 2020 by Zondervan

Requests for information should be addressed to:
Zondervan, *3900 Sparks Dr. SE, Grand Rapids, Michigan 49546*

ISBN 978-0-310-11054-5 (softcover)

Printed in the United States of America

CONTENTS

Introduction

Welcome to *A CourseGuide for Five Views on Biblical Inerrancy*. These guides were created for formal and informal students alike who want to engage deeper in biblical, theological, or ministry studies. We hope this guide will provide an opportunity for you to grow not only in your understanding, but also in your faith.

How to Use This Guide

This guide is meant to be used in conjunction with the book *Five Views on Biblical Inerrancy* and its corresponding videos, *Five Views on Biblical Inerrancy, A Video Study*. After you have read each chapter in the book and watched the accompanying video lesson, the materials in this guide will help you review and assess what you have learned. Application-oriented questions are included as well.

Each CourseGuide has been individually designed to best equip you in your studies, but in general, you can expect the following components. Most CourseGuides begin every chapter with a "You Should Know" section, which highlights key terminology, people, and facts to remember. This section serves as a helpful summary for directing your studies. Reflection questions, typically two to three per chapter, prompt you to summarize key points you've learned. Discussion questions invite you to an even deeper level of engagement. Finally, most chapters will end with a short quiz to test your retention. You can find the answer key to each quiz at the bottom of the page following it.

For Further Study

CourseGuides accompany books and videos from some of the world's top biblical and theological scholars. They may be used independently, or in small groups or classrooms, offering quality instruction to equip students for academic and ministry pursuits. If you would like to engage in further study with Zondervan's CourseGuides, the full lineup may be viewed online. After completing your studies with *A CourseGuide for Five Views on Biblical Inerrancy*, we recommend moving on to *A CourseGuide for Historical Theology* and *A CourseGuide for God's Word Alone*.

Introduction:
On Debating Inerrancy

Essay Question

1. According to Merrick and Garrett, how does the doctrine of inerrancy relate to other important Christian doctrines (e.g., revelation, Scripture, God, the Holy Spirit, etc.)? Describe how inerrancy relates to these other doctrines.

CHAPTER 1

When the Bible Speaks, God Speaks: The Classic Doctrine of Biblical Inerrancy (Albert Mohler)

You Should Know

- The Evangelical Theological Society requires the following affirmation of inerrancy: "The Bible alone, and the Bible in its entirety, is the Word of God written and is therefore inerrant in the autographs."

- Regarding the Chicago Statement on Inerrancy, "To be true to the Scriptures, I believe, evangelicals must affirm its stated affirmations and join in its stated denials."

- Important historical developments relating to the doctrine of inerrancy: the Evangelical Theological Society is founded and makes inerrancy a required affirmation; J. I. Packer's book *"Fundamentalism" and the Word of God* is published; the Wenham Conference on Scripture meets but doesn't take a position on inerrancy; Fuller Theological Seminary revises its confessional statement and doesn't include a previous statement that Scripture is "free from all error"; the Chicago Statement on Biblical Inerrancy is adopted

- Verbal inspiration: God determined the very words of the Bible in the original

- Origen of Alexandria: asserted the necessity of spiritual exegesis

- Augustine of Hippo: employed an allegorical approach to biblical interpretation

- "For prophecy never had its origin in the human will, but prophets, though human, spoke from God as they were carried along by the Holy Spirit" (2 Peter 1:21).

- "All Scripture is God-breathed and is useful for teaching, rebuking, correcting and training in righteousness" (2 Timothy 3:16).

- 1978: the year the Chicago Statement on Biblical Inerrancy was adopted

- Cultural accommodation: the practice of too closely associating the Bible and Christian faith with the values and presuppositions of a particular social, cultural, or philosophical outlook

Essay Questions
Short

1. Albert Mohler quotes an excerpt from the Chicago Statement on Biblical Inerrancy titled "A Short Statement" that contains five statements. Choose two of the statements and explain how they contribute to or challenge your understanding of inerrancy.

2. What reason(s) does Mohler give for the importance of the doctrine of inerrancy in relation to the practical needs of the church? Do you agree with him?

3. According to Mohler, what is the relationship between the trustworthiness of God and the truthfulness of the Bible? What theological affirmations and consequences does Mohler associate with a belief in inerrancy?

Long

1. Which points from the four responses to Albert Mohler's essay did you find the most compelling or troubling? Choose at least three

points, each point from a different responder, and explain your reasons for agreeing or disagreeing.

2. Mohler states that he does not believe that "evangelicalism can survive without the explicit and complete assertion of biblical inerrancy." Give at least three reasons why you agree or disagree with him.

Response Essay Questions

1. Summarize Peter Enns's critique of Albert Mohler's treatment of Joshua 6. Do you agree or disagree with Enns?

2. Summarize Michael Bird's critique of Albert Mohler's assertion that the Chicago Statement on Biblical Inerrancy is "the quintessential statement of biblical inerrancy and that its clearly defined language remains essential to the health of evangelicalism and the integrity of the Christian church." Which point is the most persuasive? Why?

3. Briefly explain the distinction Vanhoozer makes between "original" and "modernist/rationalist" versions of inerrancy. Which version, if either, do you find most persuasive?

4. What objections does Franke raise to Mohler's complete affirmation of the Chicago Statement on Biblical Inerrancy? Do you find these persuasive?

Quiz

1. (T/F) Albert Mohler holds that evangelicalism cannot survive without a complete assertion of biblical inerrancy.

2. (T/F) Regarding Joshua 6, Mohler insists that we have to wait for additional findings from archaeology before we decide whether the biblical account is historical or not.

3. (T/F) Mohler argues that a belief in inerrancy is important for theology but has little impact on Christian preaching.

4. (T/F) Mohler says that the best way to understand the alleged contradiction between Acts 9:7 and Acts 22:9 is to realize that the author, Luke, wasn't interested in these minor details.

5. The book *"Fundamentalism" and the Word of God* by _____ was a response to Gabriel Herbert's book *Fundamentalism and the Church of God*, which challenged the truthfulness of the Bible.

    a) Albert Mohler
    b) J. I. Packer
    c) Carl F. H. Henry
    d) B. B. Warfield

6. Which of the following is NOT asserted in the Chicago Statement on Biblical Inerrancy?

    a) The Bible is the authoritative Word of God
    b) Inerrancy has been integral to the church's faith throughout history
    c) Alleged errors and discrepancies don't undermine the Bible's truth claims
    d) God temporarily set aside the biblical authors' personalities so that he could communicate exactly what he wanted to

7. In his discussion of Deuteronomy 20:16–17 and Matthew 5:43–48, Mohler critiques the views of all of the following except:

    a) Kenton Sparks
    b) Brian McLaren
    c) Clark Pinnock
    d) Eric A. Seibert

8. Mohler states that inerrancy means nothing more or less than the following:

    a) When the Bible speaks, the Holy Spirit speaks
    b) When the Bible speaks, God speaks
    c) When the Bible speaks, the church speaks
    d) When the Bible speaks, the world listens

9. Peter Enns agrees with Mohler on all of the following except:

   a) Inerrancy is essential for evangelicalism
   b) God speaks
   c) God is knowable
   d) Human language is adequate for revelation

10. Kevin Vanhoozer observes that "original" inerrancy refers to the church's traditional understanding that the Bible is true and trustworthy because:

   a) The biblical writers were morally upstanding
   b) The biblical manuscripts have been well preserved
   c) God is its ultimate author
   d) It has survived all of the attacks of its enemies

CHAPTER 2

Inerrancy, However Defined, Does Not Describe What the Bible Does (Peter Enns)

You Should Know

- "As [Peter Enns sees] it, the recurring tensions over inerrancy in evangelicalism are largely a byproduct of the <u>distance</u> between a priori theological assertions about God and about how his book should behave and the Bible we meet once we get down to the <u>uncooperative</u> details of the text itself."

- According to Enns, this is the pattern we see in the Bible for how God works: that God's power is made known in weakness; that God reigns amidst human error and suffering; that God lovingly condescends to finite human culture

- According to Enns, inerrancy has been a central component of evangelicalism its entire history. According to Enns, inerrancy's definitive role in forming evangelical identity in the face of modern challenges occurred with The Chicago Statement on Biblical Inerrancy.

- The ways Enns says that God speaks truth through the ancient authors of Scripture: idioms, attitudes, assumptions, general worldview

- Peter Enns says, "I wonder too if there is not some sort of Gnosticism inherent in at least some forms of inerrancy, in which a God 'up there' saves us from a finite world too mundane to warrant God's attention."

- When our doctrine demands that we believe what is contrary to disciplined observation, what takes root is cognitive dissonance and faith crises.

- Mythologized history: a historical core that biblical writers present in mythic terms

- Three factors Enns says we must come to terms with to address God's command to exterminate the Canaanites in Deuteronomy 20:16–17: the seriousness of the moral and theological issues; Jesus's teachings about how to treat sinners and enemies; the discrepancies between the archaeological record and the biblical account of the conquest of Canaan

- Incarnational metaphor: Scripture is a collection of a variety of writings that necessarily and unashamedly reflects the worlds in which those writings were produced

Essay Questions

Short

1. What do you think of Enns's contention that inerrancy should be scrapped because it is a theological proposal that doesn't account for the true nature of the Bible?

2. Enns criticizes the doctrine of inerrancy for preventing evangelicals from embracing new developments in biblical studies and other fields. Do you believe this is a valid criticism? Why or why not?

3. How does Enns evaluate James Hoffmeier's suggestion that "Hebrew writers could use mythic language and images to depict historical situations"? Do you believe Hoffmeier's suggestion is a viable viewpoint for those who hold to inerrancy?

Long

1. Enns is critical of inerrancy in general and its expression in the Chicago Statement on Biblical Inerrancy in particular. Does he make a persuasive case for abandoning inerrancy? How does he propose Christians should approach the Bible instead of inerrancy?

2. Enns states that the Bible "is a book that tells one grand narrative, but by means of divergent viewpoints and different theologies." He also holds that parts of the Bible are unhistorical and sometimes immoral. What are the implications for individual Christians and the church if Enns's views on the Bible are adopted? Does Enns's position provide any basis for viewing the Bible as an authoritative communication from God?

Response Essay Questions

1. How does Albert Mohler respond to Peter Enns's critique of the Chicago Statement on Biblical Inerrancy? Do you find his response persuasive?

2. What objections does Michael Bird raise against Enns's reading of Old Testament narratives? What does Bird see as the outcome of Enns's approach? Do you agree or disagree with Bird?

3. Why does Vanhoozer characterize Enns's view of the Old Testament as Marcionite? How does he respond to Enns's contrast of the God of the Old Testament with Jesus? Do you find Vanhoozer or Enns more persuasive on this topic?

4. Do you agree with John Franke that "evangelicals ought to embrace the valuable work Enns is doing and learn from it, even if they do not agree with him"? Why or why not?

Quiz

1. (T/F) According to Peter Enns, the Bible is a book that tells one grand narrative, but by means of divergent viewpoints and theologies.

2. (T/F) Enns observes that one of the strengths of the Chicago Statement on Biblical Inerrancy is that it is open to new historical and scientific findings.

3. For Enns, the core issue of inerrancy is how it functions in contemporary _____.

    a) Evangelical church services
    b) Evangelical theological discourse
    c) Evangelical Bible studies
    d) Evangelical parachurch ministries

4. Enns states that an implied premise of the Chicago Statement on Biblical Inerrancy is:

    a) No one in church history has deviated from inerrancy
    b) Christians have multiple ideas about what inerrancy means
    c) Christians who hold to inerrancy will experience God's favor
    d) God as God would necessarily produce an inerrant Bible

5. Enns proposes his own _____ model of Scripture, which he argues is a corrective to inerrancy.

    a) Incarnational
    b) Relational
    c) Vocational
    d) Spatial

6. All of the following are part of the Bible's own witness to how God works, Enns says, except:

    a) God's power is made known in weakness
    b) God reigns amidst human error and suffering
    c) God superintends the writing of Scripture so that errors are avoided
    d) God lovingly condescends to finite human culture

7. Evangelical scholars such as Kenneth Kitchen, Richard Hess, and John Monson argue that the archaeological data related to Jericho:

    a) Do not make the biblical account impossible
    b) Make the biblical account impossible

c) Support the biblical account in every detail

d) Indicate that there were two separate Jerichos

8. In Enns's view, the extermination of the Canaanites in Deuteronomy 20:10–20 and similar passages shows that Yahweh is:

a) A kind and loving deity

b) A tribal warrior god

c) A wrathful but misunderstood god

d) A symbol of humankind's innate desire to conquer

9. Enns favors Kenton Sparks's argument that the Gospel of _____ reinterprets the Mosaic genocide through the lens of Jesus's message of love.

a) John

b) Luke

c) Matthew

d) Mark

10. According to Kevin Vanhoozer, Enns makes the mistake of criticizing "naïve" inerrancy instead of addressing _____ inerrancy.

a) "Hermeneutical"

b) "Evangelical"

c) "Charismatic"

d) "Critical"

CHAPTER 3

Inerrancy Is Not Necessary for Evangelicalism outside the USA (Michael Bird)

You Should Know

- Three criticisms Michael Bird levels against the American inerrancy tradition: it is essentially modernist in construct; it is parochially American in context; it occasionally creates more exegetical problems than it solves

- Three downsides Bird sees to "doctrinal fences" like the doctrine of inerrancy: they tend to divide believers; they inhibit Christian witness by assuming a default defensive stance; and they risk making the Bible, rather than Christ, the central tenet of Christian faith

- What Christians have repeatedly affirmed about Scripture over the course of history: Scripture comes from God; Scripture is to be read and studied in the churches; Scripture is the inscripturated form of the rule of faith; Scripture emits divine authority; Scripture is without falsehood; and Scripture is true and trustworthy

- Regarding the Bible, Augustine said, "Only to those books which are called canonical have I learned to give honor so that I believe most firmly that no author in these books made any error in writing."

- According to Michael Bird, some inerrantists employ the following faulty argumentation in relation to revered figures from church history: good and godly people believe what the CSBI says; John Calvin was a good and godly person; therefore John Calvin believed what the CSBI says

- The primary function of the Chicago Statement on Biblical Inerrancy: to define American evangelicalism as a bounded set; to force conformity to certain biblical interpretations; to weed out dissenters in denominational politics; and to affirm that Scripture is best studied using multiple translations

- "The law of the Lord is perfect, refreshing the soul. The statutes of the Lord are trustworthy, making wise the simple" (Psalm 19:7).

- Michael Bird says, "God does not speak erroneously, nor does he feed us nuts of truth lodged inside shells of falsehood."

- Bird holds that the truthfulness of Scripture is secured by the faithfulness of God to his own Word.

- Biblical infallibility: Biblical teachings are true and without falsehood in all that they affirm, with specific reference to God's revelation of himself as Savior.

Essay Questions

Short

1. Do you agree with Michael Bird that the Chicago Statement on Biblical Inerrancy demands a literal seven-day creation and a young earth and rejects the findings of modern science? In your opinion, does inerrancy require these commitments?

2. Do you think Bird is right that minor differences in details among the Gospels do not undermine the authority of Scripture? Why or why not?

3. How does Bird describe the difference(s) between infallibility and inerrancy? Which view do you find more compelling?

Long

1. Does Michael Bird make a convincing case that inerrancy is an American concept that isn't relevant to the rest of the global evangelical church? What reasons would you give for why churches or denominations around the world are or are not obligated to adopt inerrancy?

2. In light of Bird's responses to the three biblical test cases (Jericho, Paul's conversion, and the Canaanite extermination), which approach to Scripture do you find more persuasive—infallibility or inerrancy? Provide at least three reasons to support your position.

Response Essay Questions

1. What is your evaluation of Mohler's response to Bird's contention that inerrancy is a modernist concept and also not applicable to other parts of the evangelical world?

2. What does Peter Enns view as problematic about Michael Bird's use of "veracity" instead of "inerrancy"? Do you believe his criticism is valid?

3. Why does Kevin Vanhoozer prefer the term *infallibility* to *inerrancy*? How does inerrancy relate to infallibility on his view? How does his definition of infallibility differ from the common understanding of "infallible" in North America? Do his definitions reflect your own understanding of these terms?

4. Summarize John Franke's views on the nature and function of human language. What implications do you think his views have for how Christians should approach and understand the Bible?

Quiz

1. (T/F) Bird states that he finds very little to agree with in the Chicago Statement on Biblical Inerrancy.

2. (T/F) Bird holds that the language of revelation is accommodated to the worldview and expectations of its audience in matters of cosmology and historiography.

3. (T/F) Bird observes that the Lausanne Covenant and Vatican decree *Dei Verbum* might have wider appeal to many global churches than the Chicago Statement on Biblical Inerrancy.

4. According to Michael Bird, the international view of Scripture is characterized by a commitment to the _____ of Scripture.

    a) Authenticity and integrity
    b) Infallibility and authority
    c) Study and preaching
    d) Power and precision

5. The unity of the Old and New Testaments, according to Bird, rests in their singular testimony to _____ rather than our ability to resolve apparent discrepancies. (148)

    a) The law of Moses
    b) God's universal rule
    c) Jesus Christ
    d) The nation of Israel

6. The church father _____ held that no author of a canonical book made any error in writing.

    a) Augustine
    b) John Chrysostom
    c) Origen
    d) Clement

7. _____ believed that if we possessed the original texts of Scripture, all real discrepancies would vanish and only apparent discrepancies would remain.

    a) Cotton Mather
    b) Benjamin Franklin
    c) Immanuel Kant
    d) B. B. Warfield

8. Bird asserts that only American evangelicals use Scripture to argue against _____.

   a) Gun control
   b) Environmental care
   c) Universal healthcare
   d) All of the above

9. Bird writes that ancient historians were _____ who exercised creativity in their narratives, not modern journalists.

   a) Poets
   b) Storytellers
   c) Deceivers
   d) Revolutionaries

10. According to Kevin Vanhoozer, the Bible is inerrant because its assertions are _____.

   a) Infallible
   b) Incredible
   c) Exceptional
   d) Exquisite

Augustinian Inerrancy: Literary Meaning, Literal Truth, and Literate Interpretation in the Economy of Biblical Discourse (Kevin Vanhoozer)

You Should Know

- Kevin Vanhoozer says, "Evangelicals have come to understand biblical authority in two contrasting ways, with some emphasizing Scripture's authority for faith and practice alone ('infallibilists'), others its authority over all domains it addresses, including history and science ('inerrantists')."

- Inerrancy is not a speculative postulate, but an inference from God's self-communication in word and deed.

- What must we know, according to Vanhoozer, in order to know what the biblical authors are affirming? The nature of their discourse.

- Kevin Vanhoozer says, "To interpret Scripture rightly means recognizing what *kinds* of things the biblical authors are doing with their words."

- Inerrancy is not, or should not be used for: a blunt instrument to bludgeon people who are unable in good conscience to subscribe to the notion; a means of eliminating all biblical difficulties; a means of ensuring biblical interpretations; a means of proving the Bible to be true; a means of determining in advance what kind of truths we will find in Scripture; a means of stipulating that what matters most in the Bible is the information it conveys; a hermeneutical shortcut; and a substitute for good exegesis

- Three possible relationships between inerrancy and evangelicalism: inerrancy is essential for the unity and integrity of evangelicalism; inerrancy is inimical to the unity and integrity of evangelicalism; inerrancy is incidental to the unity and integrity of evangelicalism

- Three aspects of David Dockery's definition of inerrancy that Vanhoozer finds attractive: it is a positive statement; it says the Bible has to be properly interpreted; it argues that the Bible is true not in everything it mentions but in what it affirms

- Inerrant statement: a proposition that is unfailingly true

- Kevin Vanhoozer's definition of inerrancy: The authors speak the truth in all things they affirm (when they make affirmations), and will eventually be seen to have spoken truly (when right readers read rightly).

Essay Questions

Short

1. How does Vanhoozer define inerrancy, and what role does he see it playing in evangelicalism? What aspects of these two issues do you agree or disagree with?

2. How does Vanhoozer understand the relationship between God and his Word, and between God's Word and truth? Which part(s) of this discussion do you find most helpful or puzzling, and why?

3. Vanhoozer writes, "To interpret Scripture rightly means recognizing what *kinds* of things the biblical authors are doing with their words." How can this approach help us to interpret Scripture more accurately?

Long

1. What does Vanhoozer mean by "well-versed" inerrancy? What aspects of this approach do you find helpful or unhelpful, and why?

2. What does Vanhoozer claim is the role of the reader in interpreting Scripture? What should result, in his view, when readers interpret Scripture accurately? Would you add to or modify anything he says?

Response Essay Questions

1. What criticisms does Mohler have about Vanhoozer's treatment of Joshua 6 and Acts 9:7 and 22:9? Do you agree with his assessment?

2. Choose two points of criticism that Peter Enns made regarding Vanhoozer's approach to inerrancy, and explain whether you agree or disagree with Enns's conclusions.

3. What does Michael Bird take issue with regarding Vanhoozer's general approach to textual difficulties? What do you think of Augustine's approach to such problems, which Vanhoozer relies on?

4. On what points does John Franke agree with Vanhoozer? Do you think the metaphor of different types of maps for the biblical books is helpful? Why or why not?

Quiz

1. (T/F) The Chicago Statement on Biblical Inerrancy maintains that, due to the fall, human language is inadequate as a vehicle for divine revelation.

2. (T/F) John Calvin said that if you want to learn about astronomy, you should ask the astronomers instead of Moses, since that was not Moses's purpose.

3. Vanhoozer holds that inerrancy is a doctrine on which the gospel stands or falls.

4. According to Kevin Vanhoozer, _____ accounts of inerrancy do not ultimately help the cause of biblical authority, and may constrict it.

    a) Well-versed

    b) Poorly versed

    c) Reversed

    d) Short-versed

5. Vanhoozer says that well-versed inerrancy takes account of the importance of _____ as well as _____ for "rightly handling the word of truth."

    a) Grace, peace

    b) Truth, beauty

    c) Grammar, history

    d) Rhetoric, logic

6. Vanhoozer compares the books of the Bible to different kinds of _____.

    a) Maps

    b) Highways

    c) Cities

    d) Hotels

7. Vanhoozer writes that the term *inerrancy* is saying nearly the same thing as _____.

    a) John's language in Revelation 21:5

    b) Jesus's statements in the parable of the sower

    c) Paul's exhortations in 1 Corinthians 4

    d) James's advice to doubting Christians in James 1:6–8

8. Vanhoozer states that to interpret Scripture rightly means recognizing what kinds of things the biblical authors are doing _____.

    a) With their letters

    b) With their scrolls

    c) With their personal viewpoints

    d) With their words

9. According to Vanhoozer, the archaeological evidence for Jericho is
_____.

    a) Undeniable
    b) Non-existent
    c) Inconclusive
    d) Unreliable

10. It was the _____ who first pitted the loving God of the
New Testament against the "wrathful" God of the Old Testament.

    a) Pharisees
    b) Gnostics
    c) Romans
    d) Stoics

CHAPTER 5

Recasting Inerrancy: The Bible as Witness to Missional Plurality (John Franke)

You Should Know

- Franke says it's doubtful that most early Christian leaders would have affirmed the details of the Chicago statement.

- John Franke says, "Those who defend inerrancy do so based on an argument that it is a necessary consequence of divine inspiration, based on their understanding of God and the nature of truth."

- According to Franke, conflict and colonization results when inerrancy is combined with the idea of absolute truth as a single system of doctrine that can be grasped by human beings.

- In Franke's view, a web of interconnected beliefs is a better metaphor for biblical authority than a foundation on which all other beliefs are established and built.

- Ancient Christian leaders who affirmed that Scripture was truthful and without error but employed nonliteral interpretations: Origen, Gregory of Nazianzus, Ambrose, Augustine, and Gregory the Great

- The forms the Word of God takes: the act of revelation itself; the Spirit-inspired attestation and witness to revelation in the words of Scripture; the Spirit-guided witness to revelation in the proclamation of the Christian community

- God as being-in-act: God cannot be comprehended apart from God's actions and ongoing active relations
- *Missio Dei*: The mission of God
- Divine accommodation: In the process of revelation, God "adjusts" and "descends" to the limited capacities of human beings.
- Irenaeus: He said that while it is true and faithful to say that God is light, it is also true that God is unlike any light that we know.

Essay Questions

Short

1. What criticisms does Franke offer of the Chicago Statement on Biblical Inerrancy? Which do you agree or disagree with?

2. According to Franke, what kind of truth does Scripture convey? How does this relate to inerrancy? Do you find his approach to these topics persuasive?

3. What implications does Franke see resulting from the "plurality" of Scripture? Do you agree that Scripture is "plural" in this sense?

Long

1. What criticisms does Franke level at beliefs about, or practices surrounding, the traditional doctrine of inerrancy? Do you think inerrancy should be modified or abandoned in light of Franke's complaints? Give two or three reasons why or why not?

2. In general, Franke adopts a postmodern approach to truth and language that involves skepticism about the ability to know and express absolute truth. Do you view this approach as mainly beneficial or mainly harmful to Christian theology? Explain your reasons.

Response Essay Questions

1. What shortcomings does Mohler find in Franke's view of Scripture? What is the strongest or weakest point Mohler makes, and why? (p. 290–291)

2. What aspects of Franke's theory of Scripture does Enns agree with, and what aspects does he take issue with?

3. What concerns Bird about Franke's postfoundationalist approach to truth? Do you believe his concerns are justified? Why or why not?

4. According to Vanhoozer, how do Franke's critiques of traditional inerrancy fall short? Do you find Vanhoozer's responses persuasive? Why or why not?

Quiz

1. (T/F) John Franke believes some groups have used inerrancy to assert power and control.

2. (T/F) Franke states that his approach to inerrancy serves to establish a single normative system of theology.

3. (T/F) Franke believes that careful historical exegesis is a crucial component in understanding the meaning of Scripture.

4. Franke asserts that, for many, the _____ interpretation of inerrancy is the hallmark of true evangelicalism.

    a) Chicago Statement on Biblical Inerrancy

    b) Eastern

    c) Westminster

    d) Helvetic

5. To understand the Word of God, Franke says that we must keep the _____ distinction between God and ourselves at the forefront of our concerns.

    a) Infinite qualitative

    b) Finite sophisticated

    c) Temporal creative

    d) Partially literal

6. Franke states that Scripture functions like a _____ that effectively guides our journey into the mission of God. (p. 268)

    a) Car

    b) Flashlight

c) Map

d) Compass

7. Franke writes that by virtue of the grace of _____, we are able to know something about reality, though not exhaustively. (p. 269)

a) Fellowship

b) Divine revelation

c) The sacraments

d) Our intelligence

8. The most real world, according to Franke, is the _____ world that God will establish in the new creation.

a) Virtual

b) Spiritual

c) Eschatological

d) Upgraded

9. Augustine of Hippo asserts that if we read Scripture in ways that lead to _____, we read it truthfully.

a) Wisdom

b) Revelation

c) Confidence

d) Love

10. _____ is Vanhoozer's term for the mutual relationship between one's doctrine of God and doctrine of Scripture.

a) Complementarity

b) First theology

c) Systematics

d) Compendium

Conclusion: Opening Lines of Communication

Essay Question

1. Besides, or instead of, the four major topics Merrick and Garrett asked the contributors to address, what two or three other questions or topics would you have liked the contributors to discuss? Why?

Notes

www.ingramcontent.com/pod-product-compliance
Lightning Source LLC
Chambersburg PA
CBHW011746020426
42331CB00014B/3300